Buffalo skull taken
from a bookplate in one
of Frederic Remington's books.

Remington Art Memorial Museum, Ogdensburg, New York.

Artists in Our World

FREDERIC REMINGTON

By Donna Baker

Bernard B. Shapiro
Consulting Editor

CHILDRENS PRESS, CHICAGO

Frederic Remington in his studio, c. 1905.

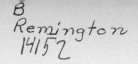

To my friend, Gene
who also happens to be my husband

Cover illustration:
  Dismounted: The Fourth Troopers Moving the Led Horses. 1890.
Oil on canvas, 34-1/16 x 48-15/16''.
Sterling and Francine Clark Art Institute, Williamstown, Massachusetts.

Library of Congress Cataloging in Publication Data

Baker, Donna.
  Frederic Remington.

  (Artists in America)
  SUMMARY: Biography of Frederic Remington,
who spent much of his life using art to document the
emerging West.
  1. Remington, Frederic, 1861-1909—Juvenile
literature. [1. Remington, Frederic, 1861-1909.
2. Artists]
II. Title.
N6537.R4B25   [92]   76-8463
ISBN 0-516-03680-7

FREDERIC REMINGTON

Acknowledgment

Quotations on pages 14, 26, 29, 30, 32, 33, 35, 37, 49, 50, 52, 57
from *Frederic Remington's Own West*, Harold McCracken, editor,
The Dial Press, 1960. Reprinted by permission of The Dial Press.

About the Author

Donna Baker lives with her husband, son, and two daughters in Arlington Heights, Illinois. Her long-standing interests in children's literature and the world of art are brought together in *Artists in Our World.* When marriage interrupted her training, which included classes at Chicago's Art Institute, she continued with private art study. Soon the love of sharing the literature of childhood with her own children encouraged her to continue her education. Mrs. Baker earned a degree in fine arts and elementary education with certification as a school librarian. She has had experience teaching second and third grades and also adults.

Her husband, a curriculum consultant, also writes for children. Travel connected with Dr. Baker's work has enabled them to visit many art museums. As a family the Bakers enjoy vacationing in the West. They particularly cherish their times riding horseback together in the northern Rockies. The author has been involved in many activities for opening up the world of books to children. She enjoys being part of that world.

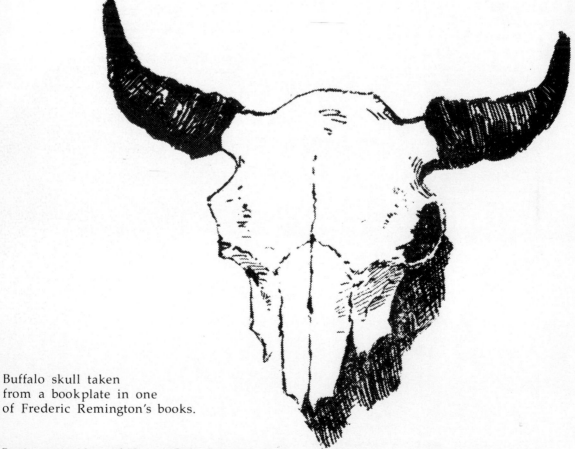

Buffalo skull taken
from a bookplate in one
of Frederic Remington's books.

Remington Art Memorial Museum, Ogdensburg, New York.

There was a region of the United States that we now call the "Old West." It extended westward from the Mississippi River to the Rocky Mountains. It went southward to the deserts of Arizona and on into Mexico. Finally, it reached northward through the plains and into the Rocky Mountains of Montana and Canada.

The Old West was open land. There were no fences and the land had not been plowed. Buffalo still roamed the plains. They moved north in summer to avoid extreme heat and south in winter to avoid extreme cold. The Indians did not live on Reservations. They roamed with the buffalo.

The Old West existed in the history of our country for about ninety years. Its spell, however, has enchanted people both in this country and in other parts of the world ever since.

Remington Art Memorial Museum, Ogdensburg, New York.

Remington and his mother.

The Old West offered a wild freedom that stirred people's imaginations. To some it offered land and a chance to create a perfect place to live. To others it promised fulfillment of a heart's desire—money or adventure.

One young man who had romantic ideas about the West was Frederic Remington. During the summer of 1881, he had been traveling around the western country. He was hoping to find a way to make a lot of money. He wanted to make his fortune, to go back East and marry the girl he loved.

In the late summer of 1881 Remington was in Montana sharing the campfire of an old man. The man was telling young Frederic that he too had left his home in New York state to live on the frontier. That was many years ago when Iowa was the frontier. He had seen the wild country pushed farther and farther west.

Now the old storyteller made his living hauling freight by wagon through the mountains to frontier outposts. He said the railroad would soon be built along the Yellowstone River. Then the wagon drivers would no longer be needed. He would not be able to earn his living.

To Frederic Remington the coming of civilization would mean the end of many things special to

Remington Art Memorial Museum, Ogdensburg, New York.

Remington's home, Canton, New York.

the West—the wild, vacant land, the Indians, the buffalo, the open range that made the cowboy into a folk hero. Remington decided he must record what he saw around him before it was gone forever. Years later he said, "Without knowing exactly how to do it, I began to try to record some facts around me, and the more I looked the more the panorama unfolded."

Remington as mascot for the fire department.

Remington Art Memorial Museum, Ogdensburg, New York.

11

Frederic Remington was nineteen then. Though he had been to college and had opportunities to work in government and business, he had not settled on a career. This lack of a future was standing in the way of his marriage to Eva Caten from Gloversville, New York. Her father refused to let her marry a man with no job.

Frederic had been born in Canton, New York, on October 4, 1861. His father had started a local newspaper, and his mother was from a prominent family. He was their only child.

1861 was the beginning of the Civil War. Seth Pierpont Remington, Frederic's father, was busy getting men for the Eleventh New York Cavalry Regiment. Then in 1862 Seth Remington sold his newspaper and rode off to war himself. Four years later, Seth Remington returned. Frederic was very proud. He later said he wanted to "be a soldier like Father."

Seth Remington bought back his newspaper. He also started training horses and racing them at local fairs and racetracks.

Horses became a part of Frederic's boyhood. Tagging along to the stables gave him a chance to study horses and learn their form. He learned to ride and to handle some of the racing equipment.

Remington Art
Memorial Museum,
Ogdensburg,
New York.

Remington at
Military Academy
in Massachusetts.

At fourteen Frederic was sent away to boarding school. He did well, but he would have liked to be back home with the colt his father was raising for him. Next he attended a military academy in Massachusetts for two years. Here his interest in drawing began to develop.

His comical drawings of officers and teachers amused his classmates. Other drawings showed his continued interest in soldiers. He drew lively scenes of cowboys and Indians. At that time, exciting stories about gun fighters and cowboys were

*Touchdown:
Yale vs. Princeton.*
1890.
Oil on canvas,
22 x 32-9/16".

Yale University Art Gallery, Whitney Collection of Sporting Art. New Haven, Connecticut.

13

"Don't write about me, just write about my pictures."

Remington painting outdoors.

14

popular with Eastern readers. Even though most people had never traveled in the West, they wanted to read about this kind of life.

The time came when Frederic's family began thinking about his future career. They wondered what college would be best for him to attend. His mother thought he should enter business. His newspaper father had always had a deep concern with politics and government.

But Frederic had his own interests. In 1878 he entered the newly formed art school at Yale. Classes met in drab basement rooms. Both the professors and the lessons seemed dull. This discouraged Frederic's new-found interest in art.

Football, on the other hand, got his enthusiastic attention. He was big and loved rugged activities. The game was still young and very rough. The players had a lot of freedom in manning their positions. Years later, Frederic Remington said that football was "best at its worst." He hoped that the game would never lose its "destructive quality."

Since boyhood, Frederic had been a natural athlete with a strength and skill that made it possible for him to excel in all sports. His natural ability, easy manner, and sense of humor made him well liked by his classmates.

Remington Art
Memorial Museum,
Ogdensburg,
New York.

The French Trapper.
1889.
Pen and ink on
paper,
14 x 10-3/4''.

Frederic became a heavyweight boxing champion at Yale. At one time, he even considered boxing for a living. But football still held his interest.

There was an especially hard-fought rivalry between Yale and Princeton, two good teams. In 1879 Frederic was a sophomore on the Yale team. The Yale-Princeton game was played on Thanksgiving Day in Hoboken, New Jersey. Ten thousand people came to watch. The two teams fought hard, but without scoring. The game was finally called because of darkness and injuries. This game was a highlight of Frederic Remington's college career.

Opposite:
The Herd at Night.
Century Magazine
April, 1888.
Dr. H. McCracken,
Cody, Wyoming.

A Run for the Scout Camp. 1891.
From *Harper's Weekly,*
January 31, 1891.

Dr. H. McCracken, Cody, Wyoming.

Amon Carter Museum, Fort Worth, Texas.

Gilcrease Museum, Tulsa, Oklahoma.

Football season was over. It was time to go home for Christmas holidays. The usually gay celebration for the Remington family was subdued that year. Frederic's father was very ill. In February Seth Remington died.

Frederic had not gone back to school after the holidays because of his father's illness. Now he decided not to return to college at all. This decision was based partly on his disappointment with his art classes and partly because of family finances.

His uncle got him work in government, but the clerk job bored him. He spent his time drawing his fellow employees while his work lay neglected. In his spare time, he continued to ride and box. His mother was becoming alarmed about his future.

During a visit to his family in Canton in 1879, Frederic went to a county fair. There he met the pretty house guest of a family he knew. This was Eva Caten. He began to court her and soon asked her father for permission to marry. Eva's father considered the young man's proposal, but decided that Frederic had very little to offer.

The disappointed Remington did some thinking. As an aspiring artist he would not be able to support Eva. So Frederic decided to go to that land he had read about and dreamed about—the West. He

Opposite top:
The Fall of the Cowboy. 1895. Oil on canvas, 25 x 35-1/8".

Opposite bottom:
Stampede by Lightning. 1908. Oil on canvas, 26 x 39-1/2".

The Cheyenne. Bronze.

INDIAN LIFE

Rockwell-Corning Museum, Corning, New York.

Gilcrease Museum, Tulsa, Oklahoma.

Indian Warfare. 1908. Oil on canvas, 29-1/2 x 50''.

The Unknown Explorers. 1906. Oil on canvas, 29-7/8 x 27''.

(See page 49, a photograph of Remington painting this picture)

An Indian Trapper. 1889. Oil on canvas, 49-1/8 x 34-1/4''.

Rockwell-Corning Museum, Corning, New York.

Indian Pack Pony.

Gilcrease Museum, Tulsa, Oklahoma.
(See page 55 which shows
Remington sculpting this scene)

Episode of Buffalo Hunt.
1908. Oil on canvas,
28-1/2 x 26-1/2''.

Amon Carter Museum, Fort Worth, Texas.

The Smoke Signal. 1905. Oil on canvas, 30-1/2 x 48-1/4''.

Ceremony of the Scalps. Oil on canvas.
Collier's, June, 13, 1908.

Register Rock, Idaho. 1891. Oil on canvas, 17-1/8 x 27-5/8''.

The Mountain Man. 1903. Bronze, 28-7/8'' height.

Dr. H. McCracken, Cody, Wyoming.

Conjuring Back the Buffalo. 1892. Oil on canvas. *Century Magazine,* August, 1892.

would make his fortune there. Then he would be considered a suitable son-in-law.

New gold fields were reported in the Montana Territory. There was also a growing cattle industry. Perhaps this is why Frederic chose to go to this part of the West to fulfill his dream. As we shall see, his fortune did not come in the way he expected.

Remington roamed the rough western land until October. He spent his time in little cow towns and mining camps. He talked with the sweaty men in the frontier saloons and enjoyed sleeping under big skies. He did not have any art supplies with him. So he drew on wrapping paper and note pads. When he returned to New York, he had a fat collection of drawings. One of the drawings, called *Cow-boys of Arizona—Roused by a Scout,* was purchased by *Harper's Weekly,* a popular magazine of the time. It was re-drawn by another artist on the staff, but Remington was given credit for the original sketch. It was a beginning.

Still, he had no promising, money-making career to set before Eva's father. When his twenty-first birthday came, he was entitled to money his father left him. He bought a small sheep ranch in Kansas. Here he continued to lead an outdoor life and to

The Scout. Oil on canvas, 40 x 27".

Scribner's, "Western Types" 1902.

sketch. He became dissatisfied with ranching and sold the land after about a year.

He moved to Kansas City. He made an unfortunate business investment and lost most of his inheritance. Still he had sold some of his pictures. So with new confidence in himself, he returned to Gloversville to ask again for Eva's hand. This time he was successful. They were married on Remington's twenty-third birthday and returned to Kansas City to live.

Dr. H. McCracken, Cody, Wyoming.

A Misdeal. 1897.

The returns on Remington's painting were not enough to support the couple. Before the year was up a sad Eva had to return to her parent's home. Frederic, on the strength of the illustration that was sold to *Harper's Weekly*, bought a horse and rode west to the Arizona Territory. Here, Geronimo was making a desperate holdout against reservation life. The West was still news.

Once again Remington spent the summer as a wandering artist. He rode across Arizona, New Mexico, through northern Texas and into Indian territory, sketching as he traveled. His portfolio soon bulged with drawings, sketches, and paintings of the frontier. He decided to return East and try to sell his work to New York publishers.

Frederic and Eva gathered up their belongings and went to live with friends in Brooklyn. Remington went from one publisher's office to another trying to sell his work. Editors were interested, but thought his work was too rough. They felt that, although Remington was talented, he needed more training.

Much as he disliked art schools, Remington borrowed a small sum from his uncle and enrolled in art classes. He went to the Art Students League of New York. This was a center for American illustration. He studied painting, life drawing, and sketching. From his teachers and other students, he gained many helpful suggestions for improving his work. He also met many other artists and illustrators. However, Remington wanted to be on his own. He left the league at the end of the session and in a few weeks was on his way back to the West.

He went in search of Geronimo. He moved through Colorado, New Mexico, Arizona, and south into Mexico. He never found the warring Apache chief, but he gained a never-to-be-lost feeling for the Indians of the Southwest and the desert landscape.

Once again he returned to New York with his work. A sketch bought by *Harper's Weekly* made the cover of the January 9, 1886 issue. This was cause for rejoicing by the young couple.

Remington still made the rounds of the publishing offices. He brought his work to a new magazine called *Outing*. It carried stories about outdoor sports and adventures. The editor of *Outing* turned out to be one of Remington's classmates from Yale. At first neither of the men realized this.

The artist presented his work to the busy editor. Without looking up the editor reviewed the drawings. The vitality of the drawings and the

"... to my unbounded astonishment ... there sat three Apaches on the opposite side of our fire with their rifles across their laps."

*The Old Stagecoach
of the Plains.*
1902. Oil on canvas,
40-1/4 x 27-1/4''.
Century Magazine, 1902.

Amon Carter Museum,
Fort Worth, Texas.

The Bronco Buster.
1895.
Bronze, 23-1/4'' height.

Rockwell-Corning Museum, Corning, New York.

". . . this phase of life so important in American history . . . is fast passing away."

authentic characters and settings caught the editor's attention. Then he saw the signature, "Remington." He began to remark that this was a coincidence he had known a fellow at Yale with that name. Then he looked up. The two men recognized each other immediately. They were delighted to see one another again.

The editor of *Outing* bought all of Remington's pictures. He also assigned him to illustrate any other stories in the magazine that suited Remington's style of work. The next year, 71 pictures were published by *Outing*. The year after that, 177 Remington illustrations were printed in many leading popular magazines.

Remington and his wife, whom he called "Missie," moved to a boarding house in Brooklyn. Orders for his work increased rapidly. His artistic success would continue to gather momentum until his death. It is unusual for any artist to become so successful and popular so quickly.

Remington was largely self-taught. He had spent five years wandering through the West becoming familiar with his area of interest. He had been to cattle roundups in northern Montana and the gold camps of the southwest. He had ridden the Oregon Trail, the Santa Fe Trail, and the other major cattle trails. He had shared campfires of Indians and the U. S. Cavalry. He had become friends with major frontier personalities. And all the while, he had been teaching himself to draw and paint the things he saw.

Now his technical ability began to improve and combine with the vitality of his style. In 1887 Remington entered works in two major exhibitions —the National Academy of Design and the American Water Color Society. He won two prizes at the Annual Exhibition of the National Academy.

"These men of nature never think one thing and say another."

A Dash for the Timber. 1889. Oil on canvas, 48-1/4 x 84-1/8".

Amon Carter Museum, Fort Worth, Texas.

Off the Range.
1902. Bronze,
20 x 20 x 28".

Corcoran Gallery,
Washington, D.C.

His work caught the eye of Theodore Roosevelt. Roosevelt had also lived in the West as a young man. Now he was writing about his ranching and hunting experiences for *The Century Magazine.* He wanted Remington to illustrate his book, *Ranch Life and Hunting-Trail.* This association created a long friendship between the two New Yorkers. Both had the same enthusiasm for the West.

Theodore Roosevelt later became the twenty-sixth president of the United States. He is noted for his measures to preserve our natural forests and waters. His interests, like those of Remington, were based largely on his first-hand knowledge and deep appreciation for our vast country.

Remington became the leading illustrator of the time. He continued to travel West with his sketchbook and his latest tool, the camera. Commissioned by leading magazines, he went on assignments to outposts as distant as Calgary, in Canada. He rode with the cavalry as they patrolled the Indian reservations in the southwest.

Remington was proud of his health and strength. Although he weighed over two hundred pounds, no one ever had to wait for him. Being a stout man, however, he always needed a stout horse.

Although he faithfully recorded the West as it was, Remington never adopted western dress. His clothing showed he was an Easterner. In the southwest he wore a sun helmet and putees, a kind of legging that went from the ankle to the knee and was fastened with straps. Sometimes he wore a canvas hunting coat with pockets bulging. This outfit on a two-hundred-pound person was a sight that never failed to make an impression. Despite his unusual clothes, Remington's good-natured face made him instantly liked around the camps he visited.

Nevertheless, the life was hard and the extremes of climate were uncomfortable. Remington took his work seriously and did the job he came to do. He faithfully recorded what he saw in his sketchbook

"No man earns his wages half so hard as the soldier doing campaign work on the southwestern frontier."

"I took ye fer an Injun." Century Magazine, November, 1890.

and his journal. He drew the ragged trapper and the disappearing cowboy. He noted details of the thankless life of the soldier and the doomed efforts of the Indians trying to hold on to their old ways.

He also collected a great deal of the clothing and equipment used by cowboys and Indians. Later he used these items in his studio to draw from. Then he could be sure that the details in his pictures were correct.

Remington gathered notes, sketches, and photographs of Indians to be used in his illustrations. To do this he wandered among the Pueblo and Navajo in New Mexico, the Apache in Arizona, and the Cheyenne, Kiowa, Wichita, and Comanche in Oklahoma.

It was difficult to get pictures of Indians. Much careful talk was needed to get an Indian to allow his picture to be taken with a camera. It was almost impossible to convince him to let his picture be drawn. Sometimes Remington would stand behind several army officers. They would talk to an Indian while Remington quickly drew the Indian's picture. If the Indian guessed what was really going on, he would go away.

Remington's writing began to accompany his illustrations. Soon he won recognition as an author

"After a long and tedious course of diplomacy it is at times possible to get one of these people to gaze in a defiant and fearful way down the mouth of a camera; but to stand still until a man draws his picture on paper or canvas is a proposition which no Apache will entertain for a moment."

as well. Many people who lived in the East and in Europe were curious about the West. Illustrations and articles by Remington, and other reporters like him, were very popular in magazines. Remington's stories and articles are still very good reading. Because they were written by a man who really was there, they tell you a lot about the Old West.

Remington was always busy. He worked for the magazines. He also illustrated several books, including a new edition of the *Song of Hiawatha*, by Henry Wadsworth Longfellow.

The Apache.   Rockwell-Corning Museum, Corning, New York.

Within three years Remington became one of the best-known illustrators of the time. He was very respected. He knew the West. In fact, people thought of him as an expert. Other artists came to him for advice on things like how a cowboy would do a certain thing, or how a particular Indian dressed.

Others preparing for a career in art asked him what to do. He wrote this advice in a letter:

> Most every artist needs schooling. I had very little—it is best to have it. Be always true to your self—to the way and the things you see in nature. If you imitate any other man ever so little you are "gone." . . . Above all draw—draw—draw—& always from nature.

Just before Remington began illustrating, the only way pictures could be printed was to use carved wooden blocks. Everything but the necessary lines would be carved away from the surface of the block. A person who could carve these wooden blocks was called an engraver. If he did well, he was considered an "artist" in his own kind of work.

This method of printing was common when Remington began his career. But shading was very difficult to show on wood block engravings. That is

Remington Art Memorial Museum, Ogdensburg, New York.

"The Apaches are Coming."
1885. Wash drawing,
12 x 17".

why many of Remington's early illustrations were line drawings. These had little or no shading.

But better methods of printing pictures were being developed. Sometime in the 1870s a new style of engraving the wood blocks was developed. It allowed some shading to be used. Little dots and lines were used to show areas of gradual changes in light and dark. In the 1880s engravings were improved by the use of photography. This new process was adopted by the leading magazines. The artists were happy with these changes. It meant that their pictures could be more nearly printed as they had originally drawn them.

Remington did not feel there was a big difference between illustrations and fine art. Being an illustrator was an acceptable profession. The people of America thought of illustrators as fine artists.

Remington wanted to be a painter, too. He did not feel his career in illustrating would prevent him from doing this. Finding the time was more of a problem. He was kept very busy with his magazine assignments. He usually got up at six in the morning, had breakfast, and worked in his

The Santa Fe Trade.
Oil on canvas.
Collier's, March 12, 1904.

Dr. H. McCracken, Cody, Wyoming.

THE TROOPERS

The Sergeant. Bronze.

Rockwell-Corning Gallery, Corning, New York.

Amon Carter Museum, Fort Worth, Texas.

Cavalryman's Breakfast on the Plains. 1890. Oil on canvas, 22 x 32-1/8".

Lieutenant S. C. Robertson, Chief of the Crow Scouts.
1890. Watercolor on paper, 18-1/8 x 13-1/8".

Pony Tracks in the Buffalo Trails. 1904. Oil on canvas, 30-1/4 x 51-1/4".

Capt. Dodge's Troopers to the Rescue. 1891. *Century Magazine*, October, 1891.

Dismounted: 4th Troopers Moving. 1890. Oil on canvas, 34-1/16 x 48-15/16".

Cavalry Charge on the Southern Plains. 1907. Oil on canvas, 30-1/8 x 51-1/8".

Through the Smoke Sprang the Daring Soldier.
1897. Oil on canvas, 27-1/8 x 40''.

Battle of War Bonnett Creek. Oil on canvas, 26-1/2 x 39''.

Infantry Soldier. 1901.
Pastel, 29 x 15-7/8''.

The Wounded Bunkie #1. 1896.
Bronze, 20-1/4'' height including base
measuring 1-1/4'' x 22-1/2'' x 11-7/8''.

studio until three or four in the afternoon. Then he would get some exercise. He either rode horseback or took long walks. Sometimes he would have to do some more work in the evening.

He continued to make trips around the country to increase his knowledge, get ideas, and make his notes and sketches. Later, he published a book that tells about his experiences on these trips. It is called *Pony Tracks*. Of course, he did the illustrations.

At first Frederic Remington worked mostly in black and white. Magazines could only print black-and-white drawings then. Still he managed to paint a few full-color pictures during the year. He kept on exhibiting his paintings.

As in his illustrations, Remington's style of painting is called "realistic." Yet, the idea we have of the Old West is what Remington believed it to be. In this way Remington is also "romantic." He shows us the Old West from his viewpoint.

Remington loved action and adventure. People in action are the subject of his pictures. He seldom painted just scenery, or landscapes. Even though he knew horses and used horses so much in his work, he was not an animal painter. To him human beings overpowered everything else.

In 1889 he entered a large painting in the Annual

Remington Art Memorial
Museum, Ogdensburg,
New York.

If Skulls Could Speak.
1902. Unknown medium.

Exhibition of the National Academy of Design. It was called *A Dash for the Timber* and was very much admired. That same year he received a silver medal from the Paris Universal Exposition for his oil painting *Lull in the Fight.*

All of his public recognition and all of his fine magazine assignments brought him a good income. He and Missie moved out of New York City. They bought a large house in nearby New Rochelle. It had nice views of the country and there was a stable.

The editor of *Harper's Weekly* decided it would be a good idea for Remington to go to Europe. Remington had never been interested in doing that, although it was the custom for American artists to tour and study in the large cities of Europe. Remington was too busy looking around his own country. However, *Harper's* had published several articles about different countries. The articles were well liked by the readers. The editor thought Remington would broaden his ideas on a European trip and perhaps get some material for the magazine.

The promise of a canoe trip down the Volga River persuaded Remington to make the trip. It would also be a chance to see the military of other lands. His friend, the editor from *Outing* magazine,

"... soldiers, like other men, find more hard work than glory in their calling."

The artist painting *The Indian Trapper.* (1889). Remington Art Memorial Museum, Ogdensburg, New York. (See page 22 for the painting)

"In my association with these cowmen, I have come to greatly respect their moral fiber and their character."

Remington's Last Painting. 1909. Oil on canvas, 30 x 27''.

was to accompany him. The canoes were made ready and shipped to St. Petersburg in Russia. In May, 1892, Remington sailed by steamer to London. He met his friend there and they went on to Russia.

At that time there were bad feelings between the United States and Russia. The travelers were not allowed to make their trip down the Volga. They waited for about a month in Europe hoping to get permission to enter Russia, but it never came.

Remington and his friend traveled through a few places in Europe, North Africa, and England. Remington visited some museums and galleries. He made some sketches and felt he had learned a lot. But he was eager to return to his own country. His friend was also disappointed with the trip. He had hoped to make Remington more aware of the rest of the world.

Soon after the European trip, Frederic Remington had his first one-man show. That is, he had an exhibit of only his work. This is an important time in the life of an artist. About one hundred paintings were shown, including *A Lull in the Fight* and *The Last Stand.* After a week, the paintings were sold by auction. His work was well liked and many people came, but the sale did not bring as much money as was expected.

A few years later Remington tried another exhibit and auction of his work. Copies of his black-and-white illustrations sold well, but the paintings did not. He began to doubt his ability.

However, new things were about to happen.

A sculptor, Frederic W. Ruckstull, came to work in New Rochelle. Ruckstull was working on a statue of a general on a horse. It would stand in front of the capitol building in Harrisburg, Pennsylvania. He had been invited by a friend to work on the beginning part of the project in New Rochelle.

There was a little group of artists who lived around New Rochelle. They were quite excited about having a sculptor in the community. Frederic Remington was among them and came over to watch Frederic W. Ruckstull work.

As Remington watched, he got more and more interested. He had never tried to work this way himself, although he admired good sculpture. He especially liked pieces about animals. Ruckstull encouraged him to try the clay. Often the sculptor came to Remington's studio and watched him place his figures in the picture as he drew. The figures were arranged to give the best view of the action. Ruckstull told Remington he was visualizing figures like a sculptor. Remington laughed, but when the sculptor sent him some clay and tools, he set to work.

All summer he worked. He liked the "mud" as he called the clay. Expressing his ideas in this new art form came easily to him. After a great deal of time and a great deal of work he finished *The Bronco Buster.* It was a clay model about twenty-three inches high.

Remington wanted it to be cast in bronze. There were special foundries for making bronze statues. Here a mold was made of the clay model. Then hot metal was poured into the mold. After the metal cooled, the mold was taken apart. There stood the bronze statue. Many copies of the same work could be made this way.

The Rattlesnake.
1905. Bronze,
23-7/8" height.

Amon Carter Museum,
Fort Worth, Texas.

The Mystery of the Match.

(Remington sketched
this actual incident.
Lieutenant Cadry,
shown in the center
with field glasses,
later died in battle.
Remington is beside
him on the right.)

Watching the hostiles from the bluffs. Harper's Weekly January 31, 1891.

Remington copyrighted his first piece of sculpture just before his thirty-fourth birthday in 1895. He proudly wrote his friend, Owen Wister, author of *The Virginian,* "I have got a receipt for being Great." He told Wister that watercolor pictures would fade and oil paintings grow dim with age, but the bronze statues would last "down through all the ages."

His work in bronze was well liked by the public and many critics too. They felt that *The Bronco Buster* was like his paintings come to life, all action and excitement. They felt he showed something that was pure American in this realistic scene.

The Bronco Buster sold the best of anything he had done. He said if people bought enough statues he would "go into the mud business." Soon he was planning a second sculpture. He was very enthusiastic about this new way of showing the life of the West. It was satisfying to work with the clay.

His business did so well that he was able to enlarge his studio and improve the stables. Yale gave him an honorary degree. With his fame and fortune so improved, he could think about things differently.

Remington traveled West again, this time he traveled for his own personal reasons, not for a

Remington Art Memorial Museum, Ogdensburg, New York.

(See the Remington painting on page 23)

Remington sculpting *Episode of a Buffalo Hunt.*

magazine. He looked at the West with the eye of an artist, not a reporter.

Though he still found the West to be inspiring and invigorating, he knew it was changing. The Indians were tame and there were brick buildings throughout the landscape. Only nature had not changed. The light and the colors were as they had been. Remington's work slowly took a new direction. His figures, which had stood out so distinctly, became softened. They began to blend with nature.

Coming and Going Pony Express. 1900. Oil on canvas, 26 x 39".

Impressionism began to influence Remington's work. This is a way of painting that deals with the way things look in light. Since light changes steadily through the day, an artist must paint quickly. Impressionists developed short, stabbing brush strokes to get the look they wanted. Sometimes light makes things shimmer. Sometimes light makes what we see seem to reflect other colors. The impressionists tried to capture such qualities in paint.

Remington began to see this way. Night scenes especially seemed to open his imagination. Many of his oil paintings began to focus on the special moods of night and moonlight.

His sculpture changed, too. A fire ruined the foundry that did his bronze work. He went to another. This foundry used a method involving wax. This made it possible to reproduce the texture of the original model. It also allowed the artist to change details before different castings of the same piece were made. Remington was very happy with all the possibilities for variety this gave him. Of the twenty-two pieces of sculpture he made in his career, eighteen were cast with this method.

Sculpture to Remington was great fun. To someone else, it might not have been, for he

"... Alas for the buffalo, and, alas, for the poor Indian too. The buffalo dance will no more bring the countless thousands of bison to the sight of the hunter."

worked long hours. He bought a summer retreat to have a place to relax. It was a quiet, wooded island in the St. Lawrence River not far from where he had lived as a child. He called it Ingleneuk. An active, busy person, Remington's relaxing was as strenuous as his working. His studio time was spent painting and writing. Outdoor time was spent canoeing, fishing, swimming, and playing tennis. He looked forward to being there more and more. Remington once said that if he could "fix up a Heaven to suit his tastes" it would be something like Ingleneuk.

At last Remington was not dependent upon illustration for his livelihood. He began to think about painting as representing ideas, not as a detailed copy of nature. Where he had used hard outlines before, he now developed forceful brush strokes. However, not all of his efforts to paint this way were successful. He destroyed many paintings that he did not think turned out well.

Some people were critical of his changed style because they did not understand the new direction his work was taking. They did not realize that by giving up strict realism, he was giving them another way of seeing what he had to say. This made details of movement felt instead of seen.

The Stampede. 1909. Bronze, 22-5/8'' height.

Fight for the Water Hole. Collier's, December 5, 1903.

Ghost Stories. Date unknown. Oil on canvas, 27 x 30".

New Rochelle was growing crowded. The Remingtons built a new place on thirteen acres in Connecticut. They had to sell Ingleneuk, but their new life in the country pleased them very much. A friend who visited enthusiastically reported that the new studio was "ideal." Remington himself felt that he was just beginning to be a real painter.

In 1909 an exhibition of his paintings received a very good response. It was felt that in the past the popularity of his illustrations had left him no time to develop as a painter. Now, at last, he had proved himself to one and all as a fine artist.

Ten days after his exhibition he was troubled with pains in his stomach. He had had stomach problems before and thought these pains would go away. The trouble grew worse. Appendicitis was diagnosed and surgery followed. But the day after Christmas 1909 at the age of forty-eight Frederic Remington died.

Remington had done what he decided to do at that camp fire in Montana. He had recorded the details of a time and place that would be no more. Beyond that, he shared with other people his knowledge about the people and the land he loved—the West.

"These Indians have natural dignity."

1855: Henry Wadsworth Longfellow writes the Song of Hiawatha. (p. 38)
1860: Abraham Lincoln elected President of the United States.
   :   First Pony Express ride between Sacramento, California and St. Joseph, Missouri.
1861: Frederic Remington born in Canton, New York. (p. 12)
   :   Beginning of the Civil War.
   :   Alexander II frees the Russian serfs.
1862: Seth Remington, Frederic's father, goes off to the War. (p. 12)
1863: Lincoln's Emancipation Proclamation declares free the slaves in the Confederacy.
1865: The Civil War is over as General Lee surrenders to General Grant at Appomattox, Virginia.
1866: Seth returns from the War and trains horses, which later becomes an important part of Frederic's life. (p. 12)
1867: Alaska sold to the United States by Russia for $7.2 million (2 cents an acre).
1869: Transcontinental railway completed, joining the Central Pacific with the Union Pacific at Promontory, Utah.
1871: The Great Chicago Fire, causing damages totalling $196 million.
1872: Claude Monet paints "Impression, Sunrise" in Paris.
1873: The first one-cent postal card is issued.
1874: A group of young French painters including Monet, Renoir, Pissarro, Cezanne, and Degas show their works in the first Impressionist exhibit in Paris.
1876: Frederic Remington sent to military academy in Massachusetts. Here, he develops his drawing skills. (p. 13)
   :   General George Custer killed in his "last stand," the Battle of Little Big Horn, Montana, in the Sioux Indian Wars led by Sitting Bull.
   :   Wild Bill Hickok shot by Jack McCall, a desperado, in Deadwood, South Dakota.
1878: First commercial telephone exchange opened in New Haven, Connecticut.
1880: Seth Remington dies. Frederic quits college and meets Eva Caten. (p. 19)
1882: War with the Apache Indians led by Geronimo in the southwestern United States.
1883: Brooklyn Bridge opened.
1884: Frederic marries Eva Caten and settles in Kansas City. (p. 28)
   :   Travels to the Arizona Territory, sketching his experiences.
1886: *Harper's Weekly* publishes a Remington sketch and *Outing* hires him as illustrator. (p. 30)
   :   26 unions form the American Federation of Labor in Columbus, Ohio.
   :   Sir Arthur Conan Doyle creates Sherlock Holmes, the famous detective, in "A Study in Scarlet."
1887: Remington wins 2 prizes at the Annual Exhibition of National Academy of Design. (p. 33)
1888: Remington commissioned by *Century* magazine to study pioneer life and rides with cavalry friends during this mission. (p. 34)
   :   Pasteur develops cure for rabies (hydrophobia).
1889: Remington wins a silver medal at Paris Universal Exhibition for "A Lull in the Fight." (p. 49)
   :   Paints "A Dash for the Timber." (p. 33)
   :   Only 541 wild buffalo left in the United States.
   :   Vincent Van Gogh paints "The Starry Night."
1890: Battle of Wounded Knee, South Dakota, the last major conflict between the Army and the Sioux Indians.

1892: Remington goes to Europe. Paints "Conjuring Back the Buffalo." (p. 26)
   : Color photography invented.
1895: The Cuban Revolt.
   : Remington finishes first sculpture, "The Bronco Buster." (pp. 31 and 53)
   : X-rays invented by W. K. Roentgen in Germany.
1896: William Randolph Hearst hires Remington to go to Cuba and report on the rebellion against Spanish rule for the New York *Journal.*
   : Marconi patents the wireless radio in Britain.
1898: Spanish-American War. The United States battleship Maine is blown up in Havana Harbor, Cuba.
1900: The Boxer Rebellion in China attempts to destroy foreign influence.
1901: Theodore Roosevelt becomes the 26th President of the United States when President McKinley is assassinated.
1903: *Collier's* hires Remington as an illustrator of full-color works.
   : First successful flight by the Wright Brothers in Kitty Hawk, North Carolina.
1904: New York subway opens.
1906: San Francisco earthquake kills 452 people and causes damages totalling $350 million.
1907: Pablo Picasso, a Spaniard, paints "Les Demoiselles D'Avignon."
1909: Frederic Remington dies of appendicitis at the age of 48. (p. 61)

Index